RECREATE SCIENTIFIC DISCOVERIES

RECREATE DISCOVERIES ABOUT
STATES OF MATTER

CRABTREE PUBLISHING COMPANY
WWW.CRABTREEBOOKS.COM

ANNA CLAYBOURNE

RECREATE SCIENTIFIC DISCOVERIES

Author:
Anna Claybourne
Editorial director:
Kathy Middleton
Editors:
Sarah Silver
Elizabeth DiEmanuele
Proofreader:
Wendy Scavuzzo
Interior design:
Eoin Norton & Katherine Berti
Cover design:
Katherine Berti
Photo research:
Diana Morris
Print and production coordinator:
Katherine Berti

Images:
All images by Eoin Norton for Wayland except the following:
Alamy
Adrian Sherrat: p. 6tr
Kevin Foy: p. 6c
Marcus Harrison-outdoors: p. 23cl
Dreamstime
Brian Mann: p. 4br
Claire Smith: 5r
Daizuoxin: p. 10bl
Lo Do: p. 29br
Lyudmyla Schloss: p. 29bc
Tania Kovats: p. 4tr
Getty Images
AFP: p. 16cl
Alfred Eisenstaedt: p. 20tr
iStockphoto
subjug: p. 19br
swaite: p. 18br
Jim Wileman Photography: p. 24tr
KSU: p. 8tr
National Inventors Hall of Fame: p. 10tr
Néle Azevedo, © DACS London 2018. Agriculture Museum, Ottawa: p. 12br
PA Archive/PA Images: p. 16tr

Pippa Houldsworth Gallery, courtesy for the artist: 24tl
Shutterstock: front cover (chocolate, stationery), p. 4c, 5cl, 8cl, 9br, 25bl
Bachstroem: p. 23bl
ChWeiss: p. 29bl
Fun Fun Photo: p. 11br
Marina Gregorivna: p. 15br
Mayakova: p. 13br
Mrs Sucharut Chounyoo: p. 13bl
Nofilm2011: p. 25br
Simonia Dibitonto: p. 23t
sylv1rob1: p. 21tl
Yasuaki Onishi M.Unal Ozmen: p. 17b
Zhukov: p. 29tl
Tomas Bertelsen,
© Rolex Awards: p. 18tr
US Patent Office: p. 20cl
Wikimedia Commons: p. 12tr
Daderot/PD: p. 26br
Yasuaki Onishi: p. 14tr, 14cl
Every attempt has been made to clear copyright. Should there be any inadvertent omission please apply to the publisher for rectification.

Library and Archives Canada Cataloguing in Publication

Claybourne, Anna, author
Recreate discoveries about states of matter / Anna Claybourne.

(Recreate scientific discoveries)
Includes index.
Issued in print and electronic formats.
ISBN 978-0-7787-5062-8 (hardcover).--
ISBN 978-0-7787-5068-0 (softcover).--
ISBN 978-1-4271-2154-7 (HTML)

1. Matter--Experiments--Juvenile literature. 2. Matter--Properties--Experiments--Juvenile literature. I. Title.

QC173.36.C533 2018   j530.4078   C2018-902457-7
                                                C2018-902458-5

Library of Congress Cataloging-in-Publication Data

Names: Claybourne, Anna, author.
Title: Recreate discoveries about states of matter / Anna Claybourne.
Description: New York, New York : Crabtree Publishing Company, 2019. | Series: Recreate scientific discoveries | Includes index.
Identifiers: LCCN 2018021347 (print) | LCCN 2018023781 (ebook) | ISBN 9781427121547 (Electronic) | ISBN 9780778750628 (hardcover) | ISBN 9780778750680 (pbk.)
Subjects: LCSH: Matter--Properties--Juvenile literature. | Science--Experiments--Juvenile literature.
Classification: LCC QC173.16 (ebook) | LCC QC173.16 .C5335 2019 (print) | DDC 530.4078--dc23
LC record available at https://lccn.loc.gov/2018021347

Crabtree Publishing Company

www.crabtreebooks.com   1-800-387-7650

Published in 2019 by Crabtree Publishing Company

All rights reserved. No part of this publication may be reproduced, stored in a retrieval system or be transmitted in any form or by any means, electronic, mechanical, photocopying, recording, or otherwise, without the prior written permission of the copyright owner.

First published in Great Britain in 2018 by Wayland
Copyright © Hodder and Stoughton, 2018

Published in Canada
Crabtree Publishing
616 Welland Ave.
St. Catharines, Ontario
L2M 5V6

Published in the United States
Crabtree Publishing
PMB 59051
350 Fifth Avenue, 59th Floor
New York, New York 10118

Note:
In preparation of this book, all due care has been exercised with regard to the instructions, activities and techniques depicted. The publishers regret that they can accept no liability for any loss or injury sustained. Always follow the manufacturers' advice when using electric and battery-powered appliances.

The website addresses (URLs) included in this book were valid at the time of going to press. It is possible that some addresses may have changed or sites may have changed or closed down since publication. While the author and publishers regret any inconvenience this may cause to the readers, no responsibility for any such changes can be accepted by either the author or the publishers.

Printed in the U.S.A./082018/CG20180601

CONTENTS

TAKE CARE!

These projects can be made with everyday objects, materials, and tools that you can find at home, or in a supermarket, hobby store, or DIY store. Some projects involve working with things that are sharp, breakable, or need extra strength to operate. Make sure you have an adult on hand to supervise and help with anything that could

MAKING CHANGES

Matter makes up our world and all the things that surround us. Water, air, metal, rock, and chocolate are all different types of matter. The list goes on and on!

Matter can change between three different **states**: **solid**, **liquid**, and **gas**. For example, we usually think of water as liquid. Water can also be a solid when it **freezes** into ice. Water can also be a gas when it becomes **water vapor**, such as the clouds in the sky.

Water vapor floating in the air

Liquid water

Solid water (ice)

CHANGES OF STATE

Have you ever seen a solid ice cube **melt** into a liquid? This is called a **change of state**. Changes of state happen all the time in everyday life. For example:

- Clothes dry when water **evaporates** into air
- Chocolate melts in your mouth or when you cook with it
- Water freezes into ice cubes and ice cubes melt into liquid water
- Lava in a volcano melts and hardens to make new, solid rock
- Water from the air turns into droplets on a cold surface

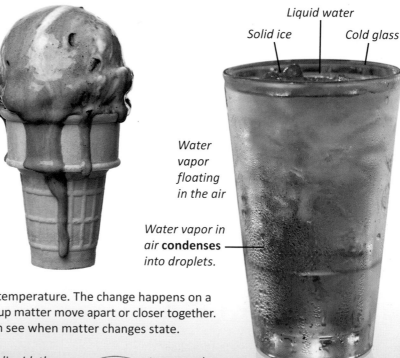

Solid ice

Liquid water

Cold glass

Water vapor floating in the air

Water vapor in air **condenses** into droplets.

HOW IT WORKS

Changes of state happen because of changes of temperature. The change happens on a small level. Tiny **atoms** and **molecules** that make up matter move apart or closer together. We can't see the atoms or molecules, but we can see when matter changes state.

 In a solid, the molecules are tightly packed and don't move much.

 In a liquid, the molecules can flow and move past each other.

 In a gas, the molecules are far apart and zoom around.

HEAT AND MATTER

As matter heats up, the molecules gain energy and move more.

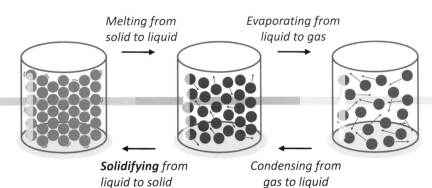

Melting from solid to liquid

Evaporating from liquid to gas

As matter cools down, the molecules lose energy and move less.

Solidifying from liquid to solid

Condensing from gas to liquid

Chocolate is melted so it can be poured into molds to make different shapes.

USING THE CHANGES

Changes of state are a big part of everyday activities and inventions. For example, **steam** power is one of the most important inventions ever. Water boils to make steam, which is a hot water vapor (gas). The change in state creates a pushing force to power machines. Steam power can also turn **turbines** to **generate** electricity. A fridge works by evaporating a chemical to remove heat. Many foods also depend on changes of state, such as dried fruit, ice cream, and chocolate.

CHANGES IN ART

Artists often use changes of state to make their work. Clay and paint have to dry though evaporation. Melted wax helps make the casts that shape statues. More and more artists also use changes of state as part of their art. For example, an ice sculpture changes over time by melting.

An ice sculpture that is left to melt in the sunshine

5

CHOCOLATE ART

Make a picture out of chocolate. A perfect birthday card!

"I could not decide whether to become a chef or an artist. I wanted to be both."
— **Prudence Staite**

Prudence Staite's chocolate painting of The Scream. *The original is a famous art piece by Edvard Munch.*

PRUDENCE STAITE

(1979–)

Prudence Staite is a food artist. She combines art and cooking skills to make paintings, sculptures, and objects out of food. Prudence makes chocolate art and other creations, including portraits and statues.

WHAT YOU NEED

- three 3.5-ounce (100 g) bars of chocolate: one dark, one milk, and one white
- small foil baking tray
- tea towel
- small saucepan
- knife
- chopping board
- three bowls that fit over the saucepan
- three spoons
- three small sealable sandwich bags
- scissors
- aluminum foil
- cake decorations
- plate

Step 1

If your foil tray's base isn't flat, rub it with a tea towel to smooth it out. Unwrap one bar of chocolate. With an adult to help, chop the chocolate into small pieces. Put half of it into a bowl.

Step 2

Ask an adult to heat some water in the saucepan until it is almost boiling. Take it off the heat and rest the bowl of chocolate over the pan. Stir until the chocolate is almost melted.

Step 3

Remove the bowl and stir in the rest of the chopped chocolate. The heat will help it melt. Repeat this step for the other two bars, so you have three bowls of melted chocolate.

Step 4

Spoon each type of chocolate into separate sandwich bags. Seal the bags. With scissors, snip a tiny corner of each bag. You can now squeeze the bags to draw chocolate lines.

Step 5

Practice first on a piece of foil if you like. Then start drawing on the base of the foil tray. Create your pictures using different chocolate colors. Use some cake decorations to add color and sparkle.

Step 6

When your picture is complete, add more chocolate to make a layer about 0.5 inches (1 cm) deep. Gently smooth the surface with a spoon. Leave your art to set in a cool place for several hours.

Step 7

Turn the tray upside down over a plate and gently press the picture out. Use a tea towel so that your hands don't melt the chocolate.

To give your picture as a present, put it in a food gift bag and tie with a ribbon. It will melt easily, so keep it cool and give it the same day if you can.

MELT AND SOLIDIFY

Even though the chocolate never gets icy cold, it still involves melting and solidifying. As a melted liquid, you can use the chocolate to draw and paint. Then you let it set or cool off again so that it's solid. The **melting** and **freezing point** of water is -32 °F (0 °C) which feels very cold. For chocolate, it is around 90 °F (32 °C).

REMEMBER

The parts you draw first will make the top layer of your chocolate art.

SUMMER SLUSHIES

Omar Knedlik invented half-frozen slushy drinks by accident! Then, he built a machine to make them. They're easy to make at home, too.

Slush drinks are now popular around the world.

OMAR KNEDLIK

(1916–1989)

In the 1950s, Omar Knedlik owned an ice cream shop in Kansas. It gets very hot in Kansas during the summer. One day, his soda machine stopped working. He put the bottles of soda in the freezer to cool down. If Omar left the bottles too long, they turned into a semi-frozen slush, which customers loved! The drinks were so popular, he turned an old ice-cream machine into a machine to make more slush. He later worked with an air-conditioner company to create a slush machine. They called it the ICEE machine.

WHAT YOU NEED

- concentrated juice, frozen or bottled
- water
- two cups of ice cubes
- measuring cup (or any average-sized cup)
- large spoon
- food processor or blender
- jug or large bowl
- drinking straws
- glass for serving
- food coloring (optional)

1

Step 1

Mix a glass of concentrated juice. The juice should be about three times stronger than normal. Ice gets added later and will change the flavor.

2

Step 2

Ask an adult to get the blender ready. Measure out two cups of ice cubes and put them into the food processor, jug or large bowl. Pour in the glass of juice, as well.

3

Step 3

Ask an adult to switch the food processor or blender on. Blend the mixture in short pulses. Keep blending until it turns into a thick, lumpy slush.

Step 4

Spoon the slush into glasses. Add straws and fruit decorations, if you like. Drink before it melts!

ICE SOUP

A slushy drink is halfway between a popsicle and a normal drink. You can't keep the slushy in the freezer because it can become rock-hard. Slushy machines keep the mixture just below freezing. They also keep the slush moving, so that the lumps of ice can't freeze together. Instead of being a solid lump of ice, a slushy has lots of small chunks of ice with some liquid. The texture is a bit like a thick soup. This means you can drink the slushy with a straw.

COOL COLORS

If you use frozen juice with a strong color, you'll get a bright colored slushy. If you use a paler flavor, such as lemon, you can add food coloring to brighten it up.

CRAYON CREATIONS

Make multicolored crayons using the power of melting and solidifying.

EDWIN BINNEY

(1866–1934)

In the 1800s, Edwin Binney and his cousin Harold Smith owned a company. They made **pigments**, also called color chemicals, for all kinds of objects. For example, they made pencils for children in school.

Edwin and Harold asked teachers what they needed. Teachers wanted cheap and colorful crayons. Pastels used by artists already existed. These options were expensive and unsafe for children. Edwin made the first children's crayons from wax mixed with safe color. His wife, Alice Stead Binney, came up with the name: Crayola.

WHAT YOU NEED

- crayons in lots of different colors
- a non-stick muffin pan
- an oven
- oven mitts
- paper

Step 1
Peel all the paper wrappers off the crayons. Break the crayons into smaller pieces. Put different colors into the spaces in the tray.

Step 2
Make sure the crayons don't stick up above the edges of the muffin cups. If this happens, the wax will overflow when the crayons melt.

Step 3

Ask an adult to heat the oven to about 176 °F (80 °C). When ready, the adult should put the muffin pan in the oven for about 10 minutes.

Step 4

If the crayons have melted, ask an adult to remove the tray and leave it to cool. If they haven't quite melted, leave them for another 5 to 10 minutes.

Step 5

Once the tray and the wax are completely cool, you can pop the new crayons out. Turn the tray over and tap on the back of it to release them.

MULTICOLOR MIXTURES

Put similar colors together to make a themed crayon. For example, create a forest crayon by mixing greens and browns. Or make a sunset crayon by mixing pink, orange, and yellow. Or mix all the colors for a rainbow crayon! Use the edge of the crayon for a multicolored effect.

MELT IT, MOLD IT

We make crayons by mixing pigments with melted wax. The liquid gets poured into molds. Then the liquid sets or solidifies. When the liquid becomes a solid, it is in the shape of the mold. The same thing happens when you melt the crayons again to make multicolored crayons.

Thousands of everyday objects use this same process. These objects include crayons, buttons, toys, bottles, and even parts of cars and planes.

A blow molding machine making plastic bottles

11

INSTANT ICE CREAM

Make your own ice cream the way they did before freezers!

WHAT YOU NEED

- two sealable plastic food bags, one small and one large
- enough ice cubes to fill the large bag
- half a cup of salt
- one cup of full-fat milk
- half a teaspoon of vanilla essence or flavoring
- two tablespoons of sugar
- mixing bowl or jug
- towel or tea towel
- serving bowl, spoon, and sprinkles

1

Step 1

Measure the milk, vanilla, and sugar into the bowl or jug. Stir well. Pour the mixture into the small food bag. Squeeze out as much air as possible. Then seal the bag tightly.

NANCY JOHNSON

(1795–1890)

In 1843, Nancy Johnson had an idea for a brilliant invention. Her idea made it much easier to make ice cream.

Before this invention, people made ice cream in a container surrounded with ice and salt. They took the mixture off the sides as it froze. This was hard work and took hours. Johnson's device had a handle that moved a paddle inside the machine. The machine constantly moved the mixture inwards from the sides while the lid kept it cold. Home ice-cream makers still work in a similar way today.

A later version of Johnson's invention

2

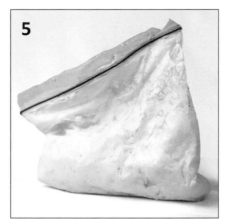

3

Step 2

Fill the large food bag with ice cubes. Pour in the salt. Close the bag and shake the ice cubes around to cover them in salt.

Step 3

Open the bag of ice. Carefully push the smaller bag of milk into the middle, so that it's surrounded by salty ice cubes. Seal the ice cube bag again.

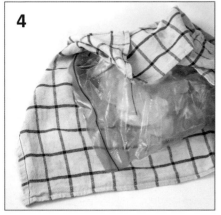

4

5

6

Step 4

Shake and squeeze the ice cube bag for several minutes. It will get very cold, so wrap it in a towel to keep your hands from freezing.

Step 5

After about five minutes of squeezing and shaking, feel the milk inside the smaller bag. It should be ice cream! If not, shake it for another two minutes.

Step 6

When the ice cream is ready, take out the small bag. Quickly rinse it under a cold tap to take the salt off. Scoop the ice cream into a bowl and eat immediately!

Try making different flavors of ice cream. You can use strawberry or chocolate milk. Milk alternatives work too, such as soy or oat milk.

SALT SCIENCE

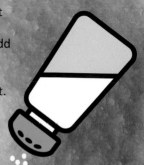

Why add salt? To freeze water, it needs to be -32 °F (0 °C). This is called the freezing point. If you add salt to water, the freezing point lowers to a colder temperature. This means the ice starts to melt.

Since melting uses heat, the ice takes the heat from its surroundings, including the milk. The temperature of the ice goes up and the temperature of the milk goes down. This causes everything to freeze quickly. The shaking helps all the milk touch the cold ice and turn to ice cream.

GLUE GUN ART

Use a hot glue gun like a freehand 3-D printer to create strings, shapes, and sculptures.

Yasuaki Onishi's 2013 work Vertical Emptiness FP, *made with tree branches and hot glue.*

YASUAKI ONISHI

(1979–)

Japanese artist Yasuaki Onishi uses hot glue in art. In his sculptures, strings of white glue drape from ropes or tree branches. Sometimes he dots the glue with **crystals**. These strings connect his sculptures to the ground. The sculptures can fill a room in a gallery. They create a mysterious landscape.

Onishi says the glue acts as a trace. The glue shows the path of the artist's movements and the effects of gravity.

WHAT YOU NEED

- silicon baking sheet, baking parchment paper, or aluminum foil
- old newspapers
- hot glue gun
- spare glue sticks
- baby oil or petroleum jelly
- roll of paper towels
- glitter, beads, or string (optional)

1

Step 1

Choose a work space close to a plug for the glue gun. Spread out some old newspapers to protect the area. On top, spread out your silicon sheet, parchment, or foil.

> With an adult to help, use the paper towels to clean the glue gun nozzle when you need to.

2

3

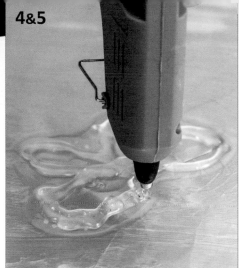
4&5

Step 4

Once the gun is hot, make patterns, shapes, and even 3-D objects with the glue on the sheet. See below for some ideas!

Step 2

Rub the silicon sheet, parchment, or foil with baby oil or petroleum jelly. This will stop the glue from sticking permanently. Wash your hands afterward.

Step 3

Ask an adult to supervise and to plug in the glue gun to heat up. Do not touch the hot nozzle of the gun or the hot glue as it comes out.

Step 5

Let the glue cool and set for about 10 minutes. Carefully peel your glue art objects off the sheet.

GLUE ART IDEAS

Snowflake

Sprinkle with white glitter.

Flowers

Add beads and glitter to decorate.

Spider web

Connect the crossing lines with smaller lines starting from the center. Add loops to attach to a window.

PRINTING BY HAND

Artists and crafters learned they could use glue guns in their work. Glue guns were an option to create objects and to stick things together. The frosty-looking glue is good for modeling water and ice.

Some types of printing work in a similar way. This Includes 3-D printing. A nozzle moves around, and hot liquid ink or melted plastic comes out. When the liquid hardens, it forms patterns or creates shapes.

Necklace letters

Make letters and add loops to hang them up.

Waterfall

Make a waterfall by draping glue over foil folded over a box or jar. When dry, position the waterfall on some stones.

MELTING ICE PEOPLE

Make little model people out of ice, using a modeling clay mold. Then let them melt or live in your freezer!

Azevedo's ice people melt in the Sun in Berlin, Germany, in 2009.

NÉLE AZEVEDO

(1950–)

Néle Azevedo is a Brazilian sculptor. She's famous for her public artworks made up of hundreds of small human figures molded from ice. They sit outside in city squares or markets. Then they melt and drip away in the Sun. Azevedo began making the ice people in place of statues. Unlike a long-lasting metal or stone statue, they represent ordinary people. Her work also represents the danger and speed of global warming. Global warming is the gradual increase in Earth's temperature.

> " The melting ice well depicts this urgency we are living in.
> — Néle Azevedo "

WHAT YOU NEED

- large block of modeling clay
- rolling pin
- rectangular plastic food container
- baby oil or vaseline (petroleum jelly)
- metal cutlery
- jug of water
- a freezer

Step 1

Roll out the modeling clay into a smooth rectangle shape, about 1.5–2 inches (4–5 cm) deep. Put the clay inside your food container. Press it down so it sticks to the base.

Step 2

Press a human figure shape into the modeling clay, using your fingers and cutlery. A small spoon makes a good head shape. Use spoon or knife handles to make arms and legs.

Step 3

Make the arms and legs thick. This will make the figure stronger and easier to remove. Press the shape deep into the modeling clay, without breaking through at the bottom.

Step 4

Use a butter knife to make flat feet to help your ice person to stand up. When the mold is ready, rub the inside surface with petroleum jelly or baby oil.

Step 5

Put the container next to the freezer, and fill the mold with water. Carefully put it on a flat surface inside the freezer. (Don't worry if a bit of water spills into the container.)

Step 6

Leave the ice person for 24 hours to freeze solid. Then take it out of the freezer. Let it thaw slightly for about 20 minutes. Then pick up the modeling clay block and carefully peel the modeling clay away.

MELTING IN THE HEAT

A solid ice block or other shape doesn't melt right away in warm surroundings. Instead, it will melt from the outside in, dripping and shrinking away.

The same thing is happening to some of the world's **glaciers** and **ice caps**. This is because of the increase in global temperatures. Some of this increase is because of humans releasing gases into the air. Gases, such as **carbon dioxide**, trap the Sun's heat.

STAND ME UP!

Your ice person should be able to stand up. If not, hold it in a standing position and rub its feet on a flat surface to make them flatter and more stable.

DESERT COOLER

Make a simple fridge that doesn't need electricity. Perfect for camping!

MOHAMMED BAH ABBA

(1964–2010)

Mohammed Bah Abba was from a family of clay pot makers in Nigeria. He later became a teacher. He developed a refrigerator out of two pots. This invention was very useful for people in northern Africa because it is very dry and hot. This invention helped people save food and lower disease. Abba hired workers to make thousands of the fridges for local families.

THE RIGHT POTS

Your two pots must be unglazed. This means they should be rough and matte, not shiny. The pots need to be the same shape, but different sizes. This is so one can fit right inside the other with a bit of space around it.

WHAT YOU NEED

- two large unglazed clay or terracotta flowerpots, one bigger than the other (see box)
- strong tape or duct tape
- old newspapers
- about 4.5 pounds (2 kg) of sand (available from garden centers)
- large spoon
- tea towel
- watering can or jug of water
- sandwich bags
- food to keep cold
- thermometer (optional)

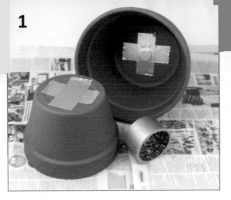

Step 1

Spread out newspaper on the floor or make your cooler outside. If your pots have drainage holes, tape over the holes well.

Step 2

Put some sand in the bottom of the larger pot. You will need enough sand to stand the smaller pot inside it with the rims of both pots at the same level.

Step 3

Start pouring sand down the gap between the two pots, using the tablespoon. You will need to place your hand at the edge of the smaller pot to keep the sand out.

Step 4

When the gap is full, slowly pour water into the sand, using the jug or watering can. Adding water will make the sand sink down, so fill in the gaps with more sand.

Step 5

Wrap your food in sandwich bags and put it inside your cooler. Dampen a tea towel and lie it on top of the cooler. Leave the cooler somewhere dry and with lots of air.

Step 6

Add more water to the sand about twice a day. You can test the temperature with a weather thermometer or food thermometer.

You should see the pots becoming wet as water soaks into them.

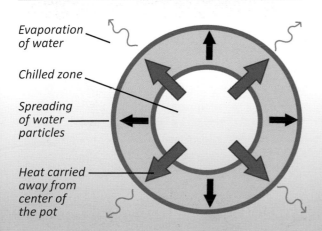

Evaporation of water

Chilled zone

Spreading of water particles

Heat carried away from center of the pot

KEEPING COOL

Abba came up with the idea using two pots, but people have known for a long time that that damp pots keep things cool.

This invention works using evaporation. As water evaporates into the air from the outer pot, it takes heat from the inside. This cools things down, the same way as sweat works on your skin. If the sand remains wet, the water keeps evaporating and the fridge stays cool. Remember, this only works well in dry conditions. The water needs to evaporate easily.

The cooler will keep working as long as you keep it damp, but it won't get as cold as a fridge. Avoid using it for food that goes bad quickly, such as meat or fish.

SAVE YOUR LIFE AT SEA

Stuck in a life raft with nothing but seawater to drink? This easy invention is the answer.

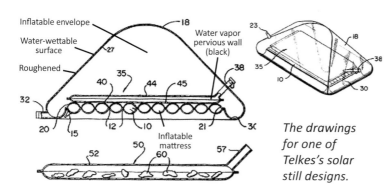

The drawings for one of Telkes's solar still designs.

> Sunlight will be used as a source of energy sooner or later...Why wait?
> — **Maria Telkes**

MARIA TELKES

(1900–1995)

Maria Telkes was born in Hungary, but moved to the USA. She worked as a scientist. She was interested in the power of sunlight and **solar** energy. She made **solar-powered** systems. This includes solar-powered heating for houses, a solar-powered oven, and **solar panels**. People called her "the sun queen."

During the Second World War (1939-1945), she worked to provide fresh water for sailors on life rafts. Their ship had been torpedoed and sunk. Her portable solar **still** used the Sun's energy to evaporate salt water. This left the salt behind and made it safe to drink.

WHAT YOU NEED

- a clear plastic dome, such as a plant **cloche**
- a clean, dry mixing bowl or salad bowl, the same width as the dome
- a small, black plastic plant saucer
- strong packing tape or duct tape
- several pieces of clean black felt
- scissors
- a measuring cup and spoon
- a pack of table salt
- water

There are several types of plastic domes you could use.

You can get a plant cloche at a garden center.

A disposable plastic salad bowl or dessert bowl is another option.

1

Step 1

If your plant cloche has a plastic hole cover, pull it off. Cover any holes with small pieces of tape, both inside and outside.

2

Step 2

Take your bowl and stick a piece of tape across the middle of it, from one side to the other. Put another piece of tape across the bowl at right angles to make a cross.

3

Step 3

Make a small loop of tape with the sticky side out. Attach it to the middle of the cross. Gently press the plant pot saucer on top, so it is above the middle of bowl.

4

Step 4

Cut out four or five circles of black felt that will fit inside the plant pot saucer. Rinse them in cold tap water and wring them out. Stack them in a pile and put them into the saucer.

Step 5

Half-fill your jug with water from the tap. Stir in about 10 tablespoons of table salt. Taste a tiny bit of the water to make sure it is very salty, like seawater.

Step 6

Carefully pour the salt water onto the felt until it is well soaked. Put the plastic dome over the top, so it sits on the rim of the bowl.

Step 7

Stand your solar still in a sunny place. For example, on a windowsill that is in sunshine for most of the day or somewhere safe outdoors.

Step 8

After an hour or two, you should see drops of water collecting on the inside of the dome. They should be running down into the bowl at the bottom.

Step 9

Carefully collect some of the water from the bowl with a clean spoon. See if it tastes fresh. It should not be salty anymore, as the salt was behind in the black tray.

PURE WATER SCIENCE

If you evaporate salty water, the salt gets left behind. The pure water vapor can then condense and turn back into liquid. This makes the water salt-free and ready for drinking. It's the same as what happens when the Sun evaporates water from the sea. When it evaporates, it falls as fresh, non-salty rain.

Maria Telkes wasn't the first to use this method of removing salt from water. The process, called distillation, was already known. Telkes's solar still was useful because it was portable and able to work at sea, even in rough weather. The tray held the salt water in place so it couldn't spill into the pure water. The still could float on the surface of the sea. It was also easy to store away in a small space.

Modern life rafts today have solar stills. These use a similar design.

MAKE IT BLACK!

Telkes's still used sunlight to make it evaporate fast. The salt water tray is black. This is because dark surfaces are better at absorbing light and heat.

WHY CAN'T YOU DRINK SEAWATER?

If you're very thirsty, drinking seawater might seem like a good idea, but it isn't! Seawater contains too much salt. Your body needs some salt to work, but you have to drink water as well to handle it. Your kidneys flush the salt out, but there isn't enough water for them to do this properly with seawater. Seawater can make the body **dehydrated**.

In 1982, American sailor and boat-builder Steve Callahan spent 76 days lost at sea in a life raft. This was after his boat sank in the Atlantic Ocean. Solar stills were some of the emergency supplies he had with him on his raft. They saved his life by giving him a small amount of fresh drinking water each day. Solar stills have saved many other lives, too.

EVAPORATION ART

Mix water, salt, and ink, and leave them to evaporate. They'll create amazing and unique art!

One of the bowls in Kovats's Evaporation *exhibition*

TANIA KOVATS

(1966–)

British artist and sculptor Tania Kovats makes many kinds of art. She is especially fascinated with the world's water. Her art includes rain, rivers, lakes, and seas. In her art show *Evaporation*, she made bowls in the shapes of oceans. She put colored salt water in each one. As it evaporated, the mixture left rings of colorful salt crystals.

Using evaporation to make art means you can't predict the shapes and patterns. The art changes over time as more liquid evaporates.

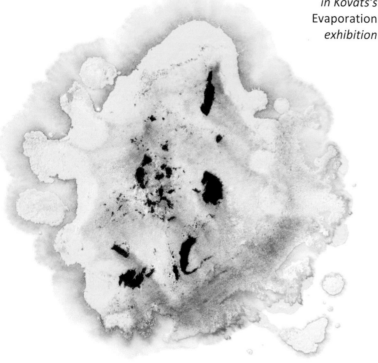

> " The sea is this enormous solvent of everything on the planet. "
> – **Tania Kovats**

WHAT YOU NEED

- a pack of Epsom salts
- small bowl
- measuring cup
- mixing jug
- large spoon
- hot tap water
- old newspapers
- water-based drawing ink or food coloring in bright colors
- large bowls
- large sheets of watercolor paper, blotting paper, or thick printer paper

1

2

Step 1

Measure a cup of Epsom salts into the jug, then add a cup of hot tap water. Stir the mixture well until the salts **dissolve** and disappear.

Step 2

Pour a little of the mixture into the smaller bowl. Stir in a few drops of ink or food coloring to make the liquid brightly colored.

3

4

5

Step 3

Spread out some old newspapers and put a large bowl in the middle. Put a piece of paper on the bowl. Press on it gently to make it dip down in the middle. Leave it on the bowl while you make the artwork.

Step 4

Use the large spoon to drip the colored liquid onto the paper. Gently spread it around to make a puddle.

Step 5

Leave the mixture in a safe place to evaporate, away from small children and pets. Check it every hour or so to see how it changes.

GROWING CRYSTALS

Epsom salts is the common name for a type of salt called magnesium sulfate. When it dissolves in water, its molecules separate and mix in. When the water evaporates into the air, the molecules stay behind. Adding ink makes brightly colored crystals.

You can try the same thing with table salt. Table salt is also called sodium chloride. The crystal shapes will look different. This is because table salt is a different chemical.

FARMING SALT

Sea salt is collected by letting sea water evaporate in the Sun. This leaves piles of salt crystals behind.

Workers collect sea salt at a salt farm in Thailand.

RECYCLED PAPER

If you have old paper lying around, you can make new paper, just like Matthias Koops did.

" The art of paper-making ought to be regarded as one of the most useful which has ever been invented. "
— Matthias Koops

MATTHIAS KOOPS

(active around 1800)

Matthias Koops was born in Pomerania, in what is now Germany and Poland. He moved to England in the late 1700s.

We don't know the dates of his birth and death, but we do know that he loved paper! At that time, most paper was made from cloth rags. There was a shortage of them, so Koops tried making his own. He used straw, thistles, bark, and wood. He also came up with a way to recycle old, used paper into new paper, which he called "regenerated paper." He then opened a paper factory to make his new products.

The opening page from a book Koops wrote and printed, using his own straw and wood paper. The book was all about different types of paper!

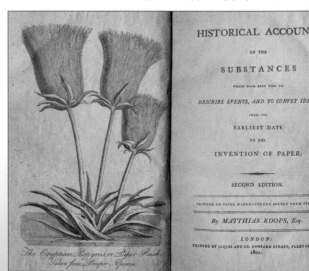

WHAT YOU NEED

- waste printer paper, newspaper, drawing paper, or envelopes
- large, wide bowl, such as a basin
- old newspapers
- scissors
- hot water
- two small, plain picture frames about the same size
- wooden spoon
- hand-held electric blender
- large plastic tray or dish
- large pieces of felt or thick cloth
- mesh
- strong packing tape or duct tape
- rubber gloves
- rolling pin

TOP TIPS

You can use most kinds of paper, but avoid shiny magazine paper or glossy leaflets. They have a coating on them that makes them harder to recycle. Look for old picture frames.

Types of wire screen you can use include:

- insect-proof garden netting
- fabric netting with small holes
- plastic canvas used for tapestry making
- wire screen used for a plastic screen door

Step 1

Spread out old newspapers to work on. Tear or cut up your paper into tiny scraps and put them in the bowl. Keep going until you have several large handfuls.

Step 2

Ask an adult to add hot tap water to the bowl. You will need about twice as much water as the volume of paper. Stir the mixture well and leave it to soak overnight.

Step 3

Ask an adult to carefully remove the glass and other parts from the picture frames. Keep the outer frames.

Step 4

Cut a piece of mesh the same size as one of the frames. Tape it in place all around the edge of the frame. This is called the mold. The other frame should be able to sit on top of the mold. This is called the deckle.

Step 5

When the paper has soaked, put on the rubber gloves. Squeeze and mush it up with your hands. Then ask an adult to blend it to a finer pulp using the handheld blender.

27

Step 6

Stir in more water until the paper pulp has a runny texture, like blended soup. Then hold the deckle in place on top of the mold. Put them both in the mixture so that some of the pulp is caught on the mesh as you lift them out.

Step 7

Move the mold and deckle onto the tray. Let the water drain out for a few minutes. Then carefully lift the deckle (top frame) off. The pulp should be a rectangle shape.

Step 8

Put a piece of felt over the rectangle of pulp, and a folded newspaper on top of that. Roll over it firmly with the rolling pin to squeeze more water out of the pulp. Lift off the folded newspaper.

Step 9

Now carefully turn over the whole mold onto a layer of newspaper. Keep the pulp and felt on it. Lift up the mold and gently pull the felt downwards away from the mesh.

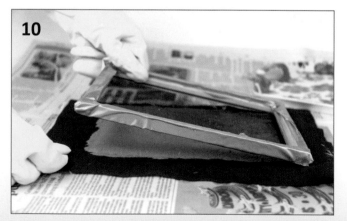

Step 10

The sheet of pulp should come away from the mesh and remain lying on the felt. If it doesn't, use your fingernail to carefully pull the corner of the pulp off the mesh.

Step 11

Leave the sheet of pulp to dry for at least a day. When it's dry, you'll have a sheet of paper!

FANCY PAPER

- Add dried flower petals to the pulp just after it has settled in the mold.
- Sprinkle the pulp in the mold with glitter.
- Stir water-based ink into the bowl of pulp to color your paper.

WATER IN, WATER OUT

Paper is made of lots of tiny **fibers** or string shapes, matted and pressed together. They can come from plants, wood, old cloth, or old paper. To make paper, fibers must get mixed with water to help the material break down. This is so that the fibers can spread out and form into flat sheets. As the water evaporates, the fibers stick together. They become firm and smooth, making paper.

RÉAUMUR AND THE WASPS

Matthias Koops wasn't the first to think of making paper from wood. In 1719, a French scientist, René de Réaumur, had an idea. He noticed that wasps made their papery nests from chewed wood. He suggested we use this process for paper-making, too. Koops turned the idea into an industrial process. Today, most paper comes from wood.

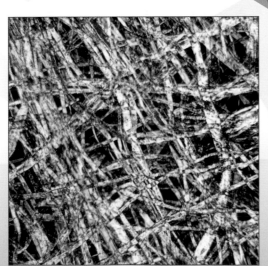

atoms The tiny particles that make up matter

carbon dioxide A gas that is produced by some types of living things, such as plants

change of state When matter changes, such as changing from a solid to a liquid

cloche A small translucent cover for protecting plants

condense To change state from a gas into a liquid

crystal A mineral that forms into a regular shape, such as a cube

dehydrated Caused something to lose a large amount of water

dissolve To break down into tiny parts in a liquid

evaporate To change state from a liquid into a gas

fiber A thread-like or string-like part

freeze To change state from a liquid into a solid

freezing point The temperature at which a substance freezes

gas A state of matter where molecules are moving fast and are widely spread out

generate To produce

glacier A slow-moving flow of ice, created by snow falling and collecting

ice cap A thick layer of ice over a large area, such as a polar region

liquid A state of matter in which molecules can flow and pour

matter The stuff that all the objects and materials around us are made of

melt To change state from a solid into a liquid

melting point The temperature at which a substance melts

molecules Units of matter made of atoms bonded together

pigment A chemical used to add color to a substance

solar To do with the Sun

solar panel A flat panel made of materials that collect sunlight and change it into an electric current

solar power Energy from the Sun that is collected and used to make electricity or power machines

solid A state of matter in which molecules are tightly packed and keep their shape

solidifying Changing from a liquid into a solid

states The forms that matter can exist in, such as solid, liquid, or gas

steam The hot gas that water changes into when it boils

still A device used to clean a liquid, by evaporating and then condensing it to remove impurities

turbine A wheel-shaped device that rotates when pushed by wind, water, steam, or another flowing substance

water vapor A term used to describe water in the gas state

FURTHER INFORMATION

WEBSITES ABOUT STATES OF MATTER

Chem4Kids
www.chem4kids.com/files/matter_intro.html

Exploratorium Science Snacks: States of Matter
www.exploratorium.edu/snacks/subject/
states-of-matter

BBC Bitesize: Solids, Liquids and Gases
www.bbc.co.uk/education/topics/zkgg87h

DK Find Out: What is Matter?
www.dkfindout.com/uk/science/solids-
liquids-and-gases/what-is-matter

WEBSITES ABOUT MAKING

Tate Kids: Make
www.tate.org.uk/kids/make

PBS Design Squad Global
http://pbskids.org/designsquad

Instructables
www.instructables.com

Teachers Try Science: Kids Experiments
www.teacherstryscience.org/
kids-experiments

WHERE TO BUY MATERIALS

Home Science Tools
www.homesciencetools.com

The Home Depot
Tubing, wood, glue, and other hardware supplies
www.homedepot.com

Michael's Stores
For art and craft materials, photography supplies, and books
www.michaels.com

BOOKS

Bow, James. *Earth's Climate Change.*
Crabtree, 2016.

Law, Felicia and Gerry Bailey. *Stone Age Science: Materials.* Crabtree, 2016.

Spilsbury, Richard. *Investigating Heat.*
Crabtree, 2018.

PLACES TO VISIT

Center of Science and Industry
www.cosi.org

Exploratorium
www.exploratorium.edu

INDEX